DOGS

A PORTRAIT IN PICTURES AND WORDS

Summersdale Publishers Ltd

46 West Street

Chichester

West Sussex

PO19 1RP

UK

www.summersdale.com

Printed and bound in China

ISBN: 978-1-84953-454-3

Substantial discounts on bulk quantities of Summersdale books are available to corporations, professional associations and other organisations. For details contact Nicky Douglas by telephone: +44 (0) 1243 756902, fax: +44 (0) 1243 786300 or email: nicky@summersdale.com.

DOGS

A PORTRAIT IN PICTURES AND WORDS

CHARLOTTE FRASER

summersdale

INTRODUCTION

Dogs hold the special distinction of being the first animals domesticated by humans, many thousands of years ago. Since then, canines have been known as 'man's best friend', offering us companionship and boundless love, from the working dogs helping us farm and hunt to the fashionable lap dogs of high society. Descended from the wild grey wolf, the dog has become a symbol of loyalty and the source of inspiration to great writers, artists and countless celebrities and people of note. From King Charles II, who loved spaniels so much that he gave his name to a breed, to the poets Elizabeth Barrett Browning and Lord Byron, who extolled the many virtues of their beloved companions in verse, we have intertwined our lives with those of dogs.

As dogs have become part of our homes and families over the centuries, we find they not only offer us companionship but also show to us a better way of living. As Tom Hayden said of the dog, 'They motivate us to play, be affectionate, seek adventure and be loyal', an attitude that can be neglected in the human lifestyle but is always embraced by our canine friends. To celebrate the dog in all its variety and beauty, this collection of stunning photographs and elegant prose, poetry and quotes offers an enlightening portrait of our faithful friend.

… in life the firmest friend,
The first to welcome, foremost to defend,
Whose honest heart is still his Master's own,
Who labours, fights, lives, breathes for him alone…

LORD BYRON, FROM 'EPITAPH TO A DOG'

Lazy as Ludlam's dog, which leaned his head against the wall to bark.

ENGLISH PROVERB

He had six or eight or more outings each day, and, owing to doors and gates being closed and to his lazy disposition, he had much trouble in getting out and in. First he would sit down in the hall and bark, bark, bark, until some one would come to open the door for him, whereupon he would slowly waddle down the garden path, and if he found the gate closed he would again sit down and start barking. And the bark, bark would go on until someone came to let him out. But if after he had barked about twenty or thirty times no one came, he would deliberately open the gate himself, which he could do perfectly well, and let himself out. In twenty minutes or so he would be back at the gate and barking for admission once more, and finally, if no one paid any attention, letting himself in.

W. H. HUDSON, *DANDY: A STORY OF A DOG*

My hounds are bred out of the Spartan kind,
So flewed, so sanded, and their heads are hung
With ears that sweep away the morning dew,
Crook-kneed, and dew-lapped like Thessalian bulls,
Slow in pursuit, but matched in mouth like bells,
Each under each. A cry more tunable
Was never hollaed to, nor cheered with horn,
In Crete, in Sparta, nor in Thessaly.
Judge when you hear.

WILLIAM SHAKESPEARE, *A MIDSUMMER NIGHT'S DREAM*

A door is what a dog is perpetually
on the wrong side of.

OGDEN NASH

Buck was neither house-dog nor kennel-dog. The whole realm was his. He plunged into the swimming tank or went hunting with the Judge's sons; he escorted Mollie and Alice, the Judge's daughters, on long twilight or early morning rambles; on wintry nights he lay at the Judge's feet before the roaring library fire; he carried the Judge's grandsons on his back, or rolled them in the grass, and guarded their footsteps through wild adventures down to the fountain in the stable yard, and even beyond, where the paddocks were, and the berry patches. Among the terriers he stalked imperiously, and Toots and Ysabel he utterly ignored, for he was king, — king over all creeping, crawling, flying things of Judge Miller's place, humans included.

JACK LONDON, *THE CALL OF THE WILD*

See a hare before him started!
– Off they fly in earnest chase;
Every dog is eager-hearted,
All the four are in the race:
And the hare whom they pursue,
Knows from instinct what to do;
Her hope is near: no turn she makes;
But, like an arrow, to the river takes.

WILLIAM WORDSWORTH, FROM 'INCIDENT CHARACTERISTIC OF A FAVOURITE DOG'

If your dog thinks you're the greatest person in the world, don't seek a second opinion.

JIM FIEBIG

And I must not forget that we had in the ship a dog and two cats, of whose eminent history I may have occasion to say something in its place; for I carried both the cats with me; and as for the dog, he jumped out of the ship of himself, and swam on shore to me the day after I went on shore with my first cargo, and was a trusty servant to me many years; I wanted nothing that he could fetch me, nor any company that he could make up to me; I only wanted to have him talk to me, but that would not do.

DANIEL DEFOE, *ROBINSON CRUSOE*

Oh, had you seen him, vigorous, bold, and young,
Swift as a stag, and as a lion strong:
Him no fell savage on the plain withstood,
None 'scaped him bosom'd in the gloomy wood;
His eye how piercing, and his scent how true,
To wind the vapour in the tainted dew!

HOMER, *THE ODYSSEY*

Money can buy you a fine dog,
  but only love can make him wag his tail.

KINKY FRIEDMAN

And can we, without the basest ingratitude, think ill of an animal, that has ever honoured mankind with his company and friendship, from the beginning of the world to the present moment? While all other creatures are in a state of enmity with us; some flying into woods and wildernesses to escape our tyranny, and others requiring to be restrained with bridles and fences in close confinement; dogs alone enter into voluntary friendship with us, and of their own accord make their residence among us.

FRANCIS COVENTRY, *THE HISTORY OF POMPEY THE LITTLE*

A Shepherd's Dog there was; and he
Was faithful to his master's will,
For well he lov'd his company,
Along the plain or up the hill;
All Seasons were, to him, the same
Beneath the Sun's meridian flame;
Or, when the wintry wind blew shrill and keen,
Still the Old Shepherd's Dog, was with his Master seen.

His form was shaggy clothed; yet he
Was of a bold and faithful breed;
And kept his master company
In smiling days, and days of need;
When the long Ev'ning slowly clos'd,
When ev'ry living thing repos'd,
When e'en the breeze slept on the woodlands round,
The Shepherd's watchful Dog, was ever waking found.

MARY ROBINSON, FROM 'THE SHEPHERD'S DOG'

The biggest dog has been a pup.

JOAQUIN MILLER

For Patrasche was their alpha and omega; their treasury and granary; their store of gold and wand of wealth; their bread-winner and minister; their only friend and comforter. Patrasche dead or gone from them, they must have laid themselves down and died likewise. Patrasche was body, brains, hands, head, and feet to both of them: Patrasche was their very life, their very soul. For Jehan Daas was old and a cripple, and Nello was but a child; and Patrasche was their dog.

OUIDA. *A DOG OF FLANDERS*

All in the town were still asleep,
When the sun came up with a shout and a leap.
In the lonely streets unseen by man,
A little dog danced. And the day began.

RUPERT BROOKE, FROM 'THE LITTLE DOG'S DAY'

*If ever the world's diplomats and arms
negotiators learn the spaniel gaze,
there will be peace on earth.*

LARRY SHOOK

Having learned to snuggle, White Fang was guilty of it often. It was the final word. He could not go beyond it. The one thing of which he had always been particularly jealous was his head. He had always disliked to have it touched. It was the Wild in him, the fear of hurt and of the trap, that had given rise to the panicky impulses to avoid contacts. It was the mandate of his instinct that that head must be free. And now, with the love-master, his snuggling was the deliberate act of putting himself into a position of hopeless helplessness. It was an expression of perfect confidence, of absolute self-surrender, as though he said: 'I put myself into thy hands. Work thou thy will with me.'

JACK LONDON, *WHITE FANG*

His hair, his size, his mouth, his lugs,
Shew'd he was nane o' Scotland's dogs;
But whalpit some place far abroad,
Whare sailors gang to fish for cod.

His locked, letter'd, braw brass collar
Shew'd him the gentleman an' scholar;
But though he was o' high degree,
The fient a pride, nae pride had he;
But wad hae spent an hour caressin,
Ev'n wi' al tinkler-gipsy's messin:
At kirk or market, mill or smiddie,
Nae tawted tyke, tho' e'er sae duddie,
But he wad stan't, as glad to see him,
An' stroan't on stanes an' hillocks wi' him.

The tither was a ploughman's collie –
A rhyming, ranting, raving billie,
Wha for his friend an' comrade had him,
And in freak had Luath ca'd him,
After some dog in Highland Sang,
Was made lang syne, – Lord knows how lang.

ROBERT BURNS, FROM 'THE TWA DOGS'

*All we need to make us really happy
is something to be enthusiastic about.*

CHARLES KINGSLEY

I am his Highness' dog at Kew;
Pray tell me, sir, whose dog are you?

ALEXANDER POPE, 'EPIGRAM ENGRAVED ON THE COLLAR OF
A DOG WHICH I GAVE TO HIS ROYAL HIGHNESS'

Buy a pup and your money will buy
Love unflinching that cannot lie –
Perfect passion and worship fed
By a kick in the ribs or a pat on the head.
Nevertheless it is hardly fair
To risk your heart for a dog to tear.

RUDYARD KIPLING, FROM 'THE POWER OF THE DOG'

Even the tiniest poodle or Chihuahua is still a wolf at heart.

DOROTHY HINSHAW PATENT

It happened that a Dog had got a piece of meat and was carrying it home in his mouth to eat it in peace. Now on his way home he had to cross a plank lying across a running brook. As he crossed, he looked down and saw his own shadow reflected in the water beneath. Thinking it was another dog with another piece of meat, he made up his mind to have that also. So he made a snap at the shadow in the water, but as he opened his mouth the piece of meat fell out, dropped into the water and was never seen more.

AESOP, *THE DOG AND THE SHADOW*

About a year ago he was first seen, a stray but by no means lost dog. He travelled about in the guards' vans, at first to stations near Lewes (where he was first seen) and then between Lewes, Brighton and London, invariably taking a train which would enable him to reach Lewes by bedtime. Then the company gave him a collar with their name on it. One day he went to a wedding and turned up at Lewes next day covered with ribbons.

BEATRIX POTTER, *BEATRIX POTTER'S JOURNAL*

I read The Odyssey *because it was the story
of a man who returned home…
and was recognised only by his dog.*

GUILLERMO C. INFANTE

The rest of that winter Bingo spent in our shanty, living the life of a blubbery, fat, well-meaning, ill-doing puppy; gorging himself with food and growing bigger and clumsier each day. Even sad experience failed to teach him that he must keep his nose out of the rat trap. His most friendly overtures to the cat were wholly misunderstood and resulted only in an armed neutrality that varied by occasional reigns of terror, continued to the end; which came when Bingo, who early showed a mind of his own, got a notion for sleeping at the barn and avoiding the shanty altogether.

ERNEST THOMPSON SETON, *WILD ANIMALS I HAVE KNOWN*

O to bathe in the swimming-bath, or
in a good place along shore!
To splash the water! to walk ankle-deep
– to race naked along the shore.

O to realise space!
The plenteousness of all – that there are no bounds;
To emerge, and be of the sky – of the sun and
moon, and the flying clouds, as one with them.

WALT WHITMAN, FROM 'THE POEM OF JOYS'

*If animals could speak, the dog would
be a blundering outspoken fellow.*

MARK TWAIN

So the dog prospered. He developed a large bark, which came wondrously from such a small rug of a dog. He ceased to howl persistently at night. Sometimes, indeed, in his sleep, he would utter little yells, as from pain, but that occurred, no doubt, when in his dreams he encountered huge flaming dogs who threatened him direfully.

STEPHEN CRANE, *MEN, WOMEN AND BOATS*

… the first knowledge of his name, proving the first cause and foundation of a friendship, which we afterwards improved and maintained, so long as God was pleased to continue us together, so perfect, inviolate, and entire, that certainly the like is hardly to be found in story, and amongst the men of this age, there is no sign nor trace of any such thing in use; so much concurrence is required to the building of such a one, that 'tis much, if fortune bring it but once to pass in three ages.

MICHEL DE MONTAIGNE, *OF FRIENDSHIP*

In times of joy, all of us wished we possessed a tail we could wag.

W. H. AUDEN

When I go out of the house for a walk, uncertain as yet whither I will bend my steps, and submit myself to my instinct to decide for me, I find, strange and whimsical as it may seem, that I finally and inevitably settle southwest, toward some particular wood or meadow or deserted pasture or hill in that direction. My needle is slow to settle, – varies a few degrees, and does not always point due southwest, it is true, and it has good authority for this variation, but it always settles between west and south-southwest. The future lies that way to me, and the earth seems more unexhausted and richer on that side. The outline which would bound my walks would be, not a circle, but a parabola, or rather like one of those cometary orbits which have been thought to be non-returning curves, in this case opening westward, in which my house occupies the place of the sun. I turn round and round irresolute sometimes for a quarter of an hour, until I decide, for a thousandth time, that I will walk into the southwest or west.

HENRY DAVID THOREAU, *WALKING*

What is so pleasant as these jets of affection which make a young world for me again? What so delicious as a just and firm encounter of two, in a thought, in a feeling? How beautiful, on their approach to this beating heart, the steps and forms of the gifted and the true! The moment we indulge our affections, the earth is metamorphosed; there is no winter, and no night; all tragedies, all ennuis, vanish, — all duties even; nothing fills the proceeding eternity but the forms all radiant of beloved persons. Let the soul be assured that somewhere in the universe it should rejoin its friend, and it would be content and cheerful alone for a thousand years.

RALPH WALDO EMERSON, *FRIENDSHIP*

DOG, n. A subsidiary Deity designed to catch the overflow and surplus of the world's worship.

AMBROSE BIERCE

His vocabulary, if it may be so called, then increases, in order to express his enlarged and varying emotions. He anticipates rewards and punishments, and learns to solicit the former and deprecate the latter. He bounds exultingly forth to accompany his master in his walks, rides, and sports of the field. He acts as the faithful guardian of his property. He is his fire-side companion, evidently discerns days of household mirth or grief, and deports himself accordingly. Hence, his energies and his sensibilities are all expanded, and what he feels he seeks to tell in various accents, and in different ways... I have seen a dog pick up a stick and bring it in his mouth to his master, looking at the water first and then at his master, evidently that the stick might be thrown into it, that he might have the pleasure of swimming after it.

EDWARD JESSE, *ANECDOTES OF DOGS*

Faithful Wully proved himself worth all the dogs in the neighborhood. Night after night he brought in the sheep, and never one was missing. The Mad Fox might prowl about the Dorley homestead if he wished, but Wully, shrewd, brave, active Wully was more than a match for him, and not only saved his master's flock, but himself escaped with a whole skin.

ERNEST THOMPSON SETON, *WILD ANIMALS I HAVE KNOWN*

Love is composed of a single soul
inhabiting two bodies.

ARISTOTLE

Presently I saw him on my right, dripping with water, cantering on at a round pace, without looking about him, homewards. I watched him, curious to see whether he would go straight home. No. He kept on till he reached the distance of about 150 yards, and looked ahead, not smelling the ground. He then deliberately walked back, catching sight of me in about twenty yards after his turning back, and wagged his tale recognisingly. He had evidently been to cool himself in the river (thirty yards to the right, it being low tide), and, thinking I would go on at the ordinary pace without him, he, after his bath, struck directly at a long diagonal for the point I would have reached if I had not turned back to look for him.

W. G. S. DOG STORIES FROM 'THE SPECTATOR'

Dog Rover shall confute you all;
Shall prove that ev'ry reasoning brute
Like Ben of Bangor can dispute;
Can apprehend, judge, syllogize,
Or like proud Bentley criticise;
At a moot point, or odd disaster,
Is often wiser than his master.
He may mistake sometimes, 'tis true;
None are infallible but you.
The dog whom nothing can mislead
Must be a dog of parts indeed.

WILLIAM SOMERVILLE, FROM 'THE OFFICIOUS MESSENGER, A TALE'

*They motivate us to play, be affectionate,
seek adventure and be loyal.*

TOM HAYDEN

The glory of friendship is not the outstretched hand, nor the kindly smile nor the joy of companionship; it is the spiritual inspiration that comes to one when he discovers that someone else believes in him and is willing to trust him.

RALPH WALDO EMERSON

Perhaps it was some celestial link with the winter night
skies that prompted the wolf to lay his song on the icy
air. For the native people who lived with the wolves,
and the wolves once ranged from the Arctic to the
subtropics, there was much to learn from them.
Is it any wonder that the myths of many tribes
characterise the wolves not as killers but as teachers?

ANONYMOUS

Laziness is nothing more
than the habit of resting
before you get tired.

JULES RENARD

She even brought anecdotes that she had heard the family and the dinner-guests laugh and shout over; and as a rule she got the nub of one chestnut hitched onto another chestnut, where, of course, it didn't fit and hadn't any point; and when she delivered the nub she fell over and rolled on the floor and laughed and barked in the most insane way, while I could see that she was wondering to herself why it didn't seem as funny as it did when she first heard it. But no harm was done; the others rolled and barked too, privately ashamed of themselves for not seeing the point, and never suspecting that the fault was not with them and there wasn't any to see.

MARK TWAIN, *A DOG'S TALE*

Ay, in the catalogue ye go for men;
As hounds, and greyhounds, mongrels, spaniels, curs,
Shoughs, water-rugs, and demi-wolves are clept
All by the name of dogs: the valued file
Distinguishes the swift, the slow, the subtle,
The housekeeper, the hunter, every one
According to the gift which bounteous nature
Hath in him closed, from the bill
That writes them all alike.

WILLIAM SHAKESPEARE, *MACBETH*

To follow for ten minutes in the street some swaggering, canine cavalier, is to receive a lesson in dramatic art and the cultured conduct of the body; in every act and gesture you see him true to a refined conception; and the dullest cur, beholding him, pricks up his ear and proceeds to imitate and parody that charming ease. For to be a high-mannered and high-minded gentleman, careless, affable, and gay, is the inborn pretension of the dog. The large dog, so much lazier, so much more weighed upon with matter, so majestic in repose, so beautiful in effort, is born with the dramatic means to wholly represent the part.

ROBERT LOUIS STEVENSON, *THE CHARACTERS OF DOGS*

'How is it, lady, that you are of such a
surpassingly beautiful colour?'
'It is natural to our family,' she said, tossing her
pretty ears. 'My mother was the Royal Crimson
Dog at the Court of the King of India.'
I bowed with deep respect and withdrew, for
I heard them calling me at home.

E. NESBIT, *PUSSY AND DOGGY TALES*

Loving friend, the gift of one,
Who, her own true faith, hath run,
Through thy lower nature;
Be my benediction said
With my hand upon thy head,
Gentle fellow-creature!

Like a lady's ringlets brown,
Flow thy silken ears adown
Either side demurely,
Of thy silver-suited breast
Shining out from all the rest
Of thy body purely.

ELIZABETH BARRETT BROWNING, FROM 'TO FLUSH, MY DOG'

Hardly any animal can look as deeply disappointed as a dog to whom one says 'No'.

JEFFREY MOUSSAIEFF MASSON

This attachment of mine to the canine family in general, and their affection towards myself, have induced me, like the Vizier in the Arabian Nights, of happy memory, to devote some time to the study of their language. Its idiom is not so difficult as many would suppose. There is a simplicity about it that often shames the dialects of man; which have been so altered and refined that we discover people often saying one thing when they mean exactly the reverse. Nothing of the sort is visible in the great canine tongue. Whether the tone in which it is uttered be gruff or polished, sharp or insinuating, it is at least sincere. Mankind would often be puzzled how to use it.

ALFRED ELWES, *THE ADVENTURES OF A DOG, AND A GOOD DOG TOO*

'T is so much joy! 'T is so much joy!
If I should fail, what poverty!
And yet, as poor as I
Have ventured all upon a throw;
Have gained! Yes! Hesitated so
This side the victory!

EMILY DICKINSON, FROM 'T IS SO MUCH JOY'

The dog was created especially for children. He is the god of frolic.

HENRY WARD BEECHER

When I call my terrier by his name,
Or join him at evening play;
His eyes will flash with a human flame
And he looks what he cannot say;
For the bond between us two
Is that between me and you!

Should a seraph sing in my ear tonight,
Or a sweet voiced angel come.
Would poor speech prove my soul's delight,
Or ecstasy drive me dumb?
For the link 'twixt them and me
Is long as Eternity.

Wide leagues our sentient forms divide
The loftier from the mean;
But soul to soul all planes are tied
When sympathy lies between;
And who shall say that the brute
Is soulless, though mean and mute?

GEORGE NETTLE, 'THE BOND'

With beauty before me, may I walk.
With beauty behind me, may I walk.
With beauty above me, may I walk.
With beauty below me, may I walk.
With beauty all around me, may I walk.
Wandering on the trail of beauty, may I walk.

A NAJAVO INDIAN PRAYER OF THE SECOND DAY OF THE NIGHT CHANT

A dog teaches a boy fidelity,
perseverance, and to turn around
three times before lying down.

ROBERT BENCHLEY

Behold this creature's form and state!
Him Nature surely did create,
That to the world might be exprest
What mien there can be in a beast;
More nobleness of form and mind
Than in the lion we can find:
Yea, this heroic beast doth seem
In majesty to rival him.

Yet he vouchsafes to man to show
His service, and submission too –
And here we a distinction have;
That brute is fierce – the dog is brave.
He hath himself so well subdued,
That hunger cannot make him rude;
And all his manners do confess
That courage dwells with gentleness.

KATHERINE PHILIPS, 'BEHOLD THIS CREATURE'S FORM AND STATE!'

We shall not cease from exploration
And the end of all our exploring
Will be to arrive at where we started
And know the place for the first time.

T. S. ELIOT, FROM 'LITTLE GIDDING'

To sit with a dog on a hillside on a glorious afternoon is to be back in Eden...

MILAN KUNDERA

'Tis sweet to hear the watch-dog's honest bark
Bay deep-mouthed welcome as we draw near home;
'Tis sweet to know there is an eye will mark
Our coming, and look brighter when we come.

LORD BYRON, FROM 'DON JUAN'

The language of friendship
is not words but meanings.

HENRY DAVID THOREAU

My dog (the trustiest of his kind)
With gratitude inflames my mind:
I mark his true, his faithful way,
And in my service copy Tray.

JOHN GAY, FROM 'THE SHEPHERD AND THE PHILOSOPHER'

So, clinging to branches and moss, you advance on the ledges
Of rock which hang over the stream, with
the wood-smells about you,
The pungence of strawberry plants and of gum-oozing spruces,
While below runs the water impatient, impatient—to take you,
To splash you, to run down your sides, to sing you of deepness,
Of pools brown and golden, with brown-
and-gold flags on their borders,
Of blue, lingering skies floating solemnly over your beauty,
Of undulant waters a-sway in the effort to hold you,
To keep you submerged and quiescent while over you glories
The summer.

AMY LOWELL. FROM 'A BATHER'

My little dog – a heartbeat at my feet.

EDITH WHARTON

The Greyhound, the great hound, the graceful of limb
Long fellow, smooth fellow, rough fellow and slim.
You can travel o'er the earth, can sail o'er the sea
But you will not find one more ancient than he.

ANONYMOUS

*Why does watching
a dog be a dog
fill one with happiness?*

JONATHAN SAFRAN FOER

When autumn smiles, all beauteous in decay,
And paints each chequered grove with various hues,
My setter ranges in the new-shorn fields,
His nose in air erect; from ridge to ridge,
Panting, he bounds, his quartered ground divides
In equal intervals, nor careless leaves
One inch untried. At length the tainted gale
His nostrils wide inhale, quick joy elates
His beating heart, which, awed by discipline
Severe, he dares not own, but cautious creeps
Low-cowering, step by step; at last attains
His proper distance, there he stops at once,
And points with his instructive nose upon
The trembling prey.

WILLIAM SOMERVILLE, FROM 'FIELD SPORTS'

*The most affectionate creature
in the world is a wet dog.*

AMBROSE BIERCE

With all the graces of his fatherland;
With well-cut coat, and ever-ready hand—
See—the French poodle sports his life away;
Obedient, wise, affectionate, and gay.

ANONYMOUS

Say! little pup,
Bark up!
Let's hear your voice.
Say, you're a brick!
Now try to beg
And do a trick.
Little pup,
Sit up!

Say! little pup,
Chime up!
Why, you can sing –
Now come with me;
Let's wash and eat
And then we'll see,
Little pup,
What's up!

HENRY FIRTH WOOD, FROM 'THE LOST PUPPY'

The Dog is black or white or brown
And sometimes spotted like a clown.
He loves to make a foolish noise
And Human Company enjoys.

OLIVER HEREFORD, FROM 'DOG'

One warm summer evening, the family was sitting on the front steps, after a refreshing shower of rain, when Whiskie saw a cat in the street, picking its dainty way among the little puddles of water. With a muttered curse he dashed after the cat without discovering, until within a few feet of it, that it was the cat who belonged to him. He tried to stop himself in his impetuous career, he put on all his brakes, literally skimming along the street railway-track as if he were out simply for a slide, passing the cat, who gave him a half-contemptuous, half-pitying look; and then, after inspecting the sky to see if the rain was really over and how the wind was, he came back to his place between the father and The Boy as if it were all a matter of course and of every-day occurrence. But he knew they were laughing at him; and if ever a dog felt sheepish, and looked sheepish—if ever a dog said, 'What an idiot I've made of myself!' Whiskie was that dog.

LAURENCE HUTTON, *A BOY I KNEW AND FOUR DOGS*

I look into your great brown eyes,
Where love and loyal homage shine,
And wonder where the difference lies
Between your soul and mine!

For all the good that I have found
Within myself or human kind,
Hath royally informed and crowned
Your gentle heart and mind.

I scan the whole broad earth around
For that one heart which, leal and true,
Bears friendship without end or bound,
And find the prize in you.

J. G. HOLLAND, FROM 'TO MY DOG BLANCO'

*Dogs lead a nice life. You never see
a dog with a wristwatch.*

GEORGE CARLIN

Funniest little feller
You'd ever want to see!
Browner 'an the brownest leaf
In the autumn tree.
Shortest little bow legs!
Jes' barely touch the floor—
And long—b'gosh, the longest dog
I ever seen afore!

But he's mighty amusin',
For all 'at he's so queer,
Eyes so mighty solemn,
Askin' like an' clear,
And when he puts his paws up
Head stuck on one side—
Jes' naturally love every hair
In his durn Dutch hide.

ALICE GILL FERGUSON, 'THAT THERE LONG DOG'

When living seems but little worth
And all things go awry,
I close the door, we journey forth—
My dog and I!

For books and pen we leave behind,
But little careth he,
His one great joy in life is just
To be with me.

He notes by just one upward glance
My mental attitude,
As on we go past laughing stream
And singing wood.

ALICE J. CLEATOR, FROM 'MY DOG AND I'

If I was sad, then he had grief, as well—
Seeking my hands with soft insistent paw,
Searching my face with anxious eyes that saw
More than my halting, human speech could tell;
Eyes wide with wisdom, fine, compassionate—
Dear, loyal one, that knew not wrong nor hate.
If I made merry—then how he would strive
To show his joy; 'Good master, let's to play,
The world is ours,' that gladsome bark would say;
'Just yours and mine—'tis fun to be alive!'
Our world... four walls above the city's din,
My crutch the bar that ever held us in.

MERIBAH ABBOT, FROM 'THE BEST FRIEND'

If you're interested in finding out more about
our books, find us on Facebook at
Summersdale Publishers
and follow us on Twitter at
@Summersdale.

www.summersdale.com